WITHDRAWN

Figure and Field

A National Council on the Arts Selection

The University of North Carolina Press
Chapel Hill
1970

Figure and Field
Jean Farley

Contemporary Poetry Series

Copyright © 1950, 1951, 1953, 1964, 1965, 1966, 1967, 1968, 1969, 1970
by Jean Farley
All rights reserved
Manufactured in the United States of America
Printed by Braun-Brumfield, Inc., Ann Arbor, Michigan
Standard Book Number 8078-1132-7
Library of Congress Catalog Card Number 70-97013

Some of the poems in this volume have previously appeared in *The Hollins Critic*, *The Hopkins Review*, *Kenyon Review*, *Michigan Quarterly Review*, *The Nation*, *New Yorker*, *Poetry*, *Poetry Northwest*, *Prairie Schooner*, *The Reporter*, *Sewanee Review*, *Shenandoah*, *Southern Poetry Review*, *Southern Review*, *Southern Writing in the Sixties: Poetry*, *The Hollins Poets*, *The Greensboro Reader*, and *The Now Voices*.

For
Jean Clark Farley
and in memory of
David LaBauve Farley, Sr.

Contents

PART I
   JANUARY   3
   GADFLY   4
   NIGHT RIDERS   6
   SCROLL   7
   NGUYEN VAN TROI   8
   THE LANGUAGE OF FLOWERS   9
   SHENANDOAH   10
   A QUALITY OF LIGHT   11
   CHARITY PERFORMANCE   12
   ELEUSIS   13
   A BETTER MOUSETRAP   14
   NOVEMBER, 1964, ONE YEAR AFTER THE ASSASSINATION   15
   STAND STABLE HERE   16

PART II
   BAUCIS & PHILEMON   19
   SHIPS GATHERED TO RESCUE   20
   GREGORIUS IN INSULA   21
   LIKE PINOCCHIO   22
   AWAY   23
   A WORLD OF WATCHFULNESS   24
   THE NIGHT HORSE   25

DAYBREAK   26
FROG IN EARLY FALL   27
CARDINAL   28
FILM   29
COMFORT   30
SNOW BLINDNESS   31

PART III
WHO ONCE KEPT STORE   35
PRODIGAL SON   37
ANALOGUES OF A JUROR   38
SHE SEES PALLBEARERS COMING ON SNOW   39
NEAR BUT WHO?   40
KORÊ TO COED   42
AT BAY   43
BED RIDER   44
FALL PLANTING   45
EMINENCE IN AUCTION HALL   47
CATHEDRAL TOWN   48
LONG VOYAGE HOME   49
THUS EVER TO TYRANTS   51
NOWHERE   52

Part I

JANUARY

In this hunched season
When purveyors are groaning with malice
Behind chimerical smiles
Of nothing plotted, nothing won,
When tall buildings weave the wind
Of a cold and boulderous sky,
And the lichened winter park of the sun
Easily overrides this lowland sty
Where our deeds of undoing are never done—

Everyone lives in imagination,
Keeps an eye upon the summit
And the wheel upon the road
Which flows as well as any frozen Hudson,
Delaware, Potomac, or James
Through detours of a million drains
Droning, "I have pumped out thy substance
With my steel snout—but will restore it
With such diversity of matter
As may thy crabbéd life maintain."

Take, eat, abscond where we may,
The real world still lies at our feet
Twisted in words and flesh—
Our old companion, begging for the wand.

GADFLY

> *"If Saigon by day is like a PX, at night, with flares overhead, it is like a World's Fair or Exposition in some hick American city."*
> — Mary McCarthy

Mortal, wordy, and trivially loathesome
As the slippery cheese brought into the house
By a sly, generous, vicious old aunt,
A seething mound of microscopic life
Who has the incredible steadiness
To sit and stare,
I take myself out to the open air
Of a wooded hillside, last rural verge
Of the mouth of the Shenandoah Valley
Before it chokes on Roanoke, that hick city:
Woods where mushrooms grow,
Where dumpsters of cans and rubbish go,
Where once a murderer found at last,
On bed of leaves, ease from his corpse.

A jet, coming in low,
Shrivels blue sky above.
Five times a day it flows on the air
From New York, that great city;
Five times a day, high tailed gadfly,
It stoops to bucolic land, bites and flies,
But still cow Susie lies,
Her great flank heaving in the sun,
Half unaware that something is being done.

Mary McCarthy, observer in the eye
Of such a fly, writes to New York
Of riding the daily Caravelle
From Bangkok to Saigon,
Of looking down from cocktails in the sky
To a Vietnamese hillside burning brightly

In the sun *like a summer forest fire,*
Can hardly believe the bombers have stooped and run
Leaving the hill ablaze
Beneath the Caravelle's peaceable gaze—
While minutely far below
A few of the hicks of Asia gape
As terror comes to birth, expected,
But born as innocent as a monstrous baby
On a clear blue day.

Restless, tentative, armed to read,
I settle briefly at the base of a tree.
A soldier stares from the front page,
Sleeves rolled up, helmet gone askew,
Holding in American arms a Vietnamese child
With black grains like pepper
Imbedded in her face.
They stare from their tilting, crumbling ledge
Of exhaustion and pain,
Easily held at bay by the camera
And hopelessly mired in newspaper grey:
Hicks, hicks, the rubbish of power,
Their temporary faces pocked
With the sign of the wandering fly.

NIGHT RIDERS

The massive trembling of late dusk air
Has drawn me from my house on this low hill:
A line of helicopters droning south
Rides one by one on the dark hump
Of eastern woods. More and more coming,
They strut their huge exoskeletal forms
In the waning light, flash
A shifting mathematical sequence
Of pale green lights.
Their rumble disposes all that is left of the day.

An invisible sack, coarse enough to stand alive,
Settles upon me, leaving holes for eyes.
I ride into night on the cover of an old well,
A raft of heavy weathered boards
Which warm my weight with residual sun
As I lie down to watch the sky.
The stars are out; a new moon sails
Overhead with the old moon in her arms.
Miles to the south those whetting blades
Sidle incredibly on a mild sky.

SCROLL

When low mild layers of earth-round wind
Unfurl the inner, lull the outer skin—
The trees of distant war, as in a dream,
Are very green, unpredictable of limb,
A little pressed for space, jostling
Triumphant as emblems
Above a march that will never start.
The fusillade which must sound there
Rolls back upon itself in air
And there in the grey green river valley
Which creases the other side of the world
Ten or a thousand soldiers hear
With a single ear
That peculiar snap which takes the quirk
From their curvature of time.
They are rolled up, fastened,
And set aside now, sadly
As an ancient Chinese river scroll:
None of their blood seeps to the spine.

NGUYEN VAN TROI

A very young man among many, quite thin,
In loose white pants and shirt:
Soldiers hold him straight to the center of the field,
Tie his elbows behind his back,
Include the pole with him.
Released to this new backbone,
His hands rise on what arm is left.
A soldier loose on the wind of a vacant moment
Catches his hand in a final touch;
Another lifts the oval black pad
To seal his eyes carefully shut
On whatever he holds in his head.
They leave him; the field in silence
Floats the young man on his slender pole;
When bullets come it cannot hold him up.

THE LANGUAGE OF FLOWERS

The finest flowers of the grave
Are plastic roses so firmly red
They never curl or crave
Any commerce with the dead;

Nor privately leach their strength
To divide and glory and multiply
From the works of that swollen trench
Too easily pierced by the mourner's eye.

Steadfast and incorruptibly pure,
They advise all summer long
Of the death which living flesh obscured:
The shameful flowering now is gone.

SHENANDOAH

    Thousands drive glinting home from work
In the late bright sunlight of October,
Leafing images of a woman vanished last night
From the city, found early this morning, strangled,
Naked, smouldering, close at hand:
    Where valley farmland, every blade shining
In slanting sun, still feeds the brotherly steer
Among quick red roads and brickwork
Of a newly fallen sister field;
    Where long reaches of maple and oak
Still wind along creeks to the city line,
Lifting, light, great scarlet burdens
That ripple the air like a silken cloak;
    Where the more wasted the borderland, once wooded,
The bigger grow the pithy weeds
Which support in their yellow autumn
Chittering sparrows that spread the seed;
    Where rough unworkable mountains hump above houses
In deep blue regions of hope,
Bundling their rude forbidden hoards
In the ancient, seamless, indifferent cloak.

A QUALITY OF LIGHT

The Spies of Israel Overlook Canaan

Far behind them lies easy the amazing sea
Where surely this day the ships are deft
Among shining curls of fleece.
Inland the light strikes clean
—As eagle to angular lamb—
On the craggy face of every man.
They mark among lustrous leaves the grapes are red
And hope overtakes them while they breathe,
Clasping thick feet in thin hands.
Set with eyes like golden seed,
Picked by sunlight from each shaggy head,
They glance afield over all their future,
Searching the place in a chosen land
For God's clear mercy on a murmurous band.

CHARITY PERFORMANCE

> *"The eleven year old Siamese twins from San Francisco, who have dedicated their talents to God, will sing tonight at the Second Baptist Church."*
> —Hattiesburg (Miss.) *American*

Into a silence as stiff as greed
Intrude two wary heads.
Avoiding the puckered faces
Which burst into flower before them,
They watch the hidden spaces
For something as reticent, say,
As a small green head—
A weaving, doubling deed in their path
Signing, I am the snake and the grass;
This steady golden eye,
No more knowing than known,
Is the crystal of perfect flesh
Which all of us bear.
Watch courteously there until, outside
Or inside, creatures may sing in their grass;
You in your sunshine
And I in my shade
Will be the two sides of Siamese twins,
Eleven years old from San Francisco,
To whom nothing in the world is strange.

ELEUSIS

Under impenetrable sun
The far hills humped toward choking
In layer upon layer of heat.
A few herbs flicked like tongues
Through white powder streaks,
And I, clambering by the shore,
Passed a giant lime works
Where five men strained
To shake from endless sacks
The dust which that dry land absorbed
Like rain.

Feet, hands, and haphazard rags,
These slowly flapping men
Were crusted with powder scabs;
Each face was thickly piled
Like sponge or fur
To follow my inching by
As an eyeless surface
Will oscillate to skim
Some faint, hopeful essence from wave
Or wind.

And all before us lived, lapping,
In cool ease
The clearest of salt blue seas.

A BETTER MOUSETRAP

Cloo, cloo, cloo is said softly
But no one hears it,
For of course pigeons live in the eaves.
Cleep, cleep, cleep is said quickly
But no one hears it,
For of course sparrows live in the trees.
Paper headed chickens hang by their feet
Above a counter of half frozen seafood
And of course their blood doesn't drip
On the lobsters with pegs in their claws.
Tree squares and row house
Are braided into an asphalt street
With now and then the glitter
Of a mortared mica chip.
A crusty fretwork of steel
Braces up the subway walls
And clamps a five trestled bridge
Down upon a dull grey river
Which sucks at an orange peel
With the mouth of a half crushed mouse.

NOVEMBER, 1964, ONE YEAR AFTER THE ASSASSINATION

Black water pooled among gentle hills
Of pasture and woods. Calling, calling,
I round the end of the little pond,
All surface, glittering in sunlight.
An Angus cow, far from the herd
With her first black lamb of a calf,
Watches me steadily. Grass shines,
The air is still. This narrow embankment
Steeply falls to undisturbed water.
If my child has seen the newborn calf
And come this forbidden way,
If the cow has stiffened toward her a step or two—
Blackening leaves shelve into deeper water.
A little girl without skill would make
No noise of drowning; her face would writhe
An inch beneath the clear, unbreakable
Surface of terror, until she shrinks
To the dark floor where life goes on in threads.
Water glitters, I run up the hill.
Only my shouts surface in quiet woods,
Full of sunlight and floored with leaves.

* * * *

No, she did not drown; I found her
After running up many hills, searching for a fear
I could not find, dark, glittering, elusive.
It is November and the pool remains,
All surface, estranged from everything
In air around, yet how easily this year
I circle down to dread,
To this pool where I came dazed
By Kennedy's shattered head.

STAND STABLE HERE

In willow by small water
Whipped by November wind
The last of the narrow leaves hang on
Like a school of minnows, darting headlong,
Constantly in place, into the eloquent water
At the foot of a rock.

One freshly fallen leaf
Comes lightly curved, almost untouching
The long slow waters of a deeper pool,
At the rock is hastened, wrenched around,
A small boat with its summer helmsman
Suddenly revoked.

And the water itself rounds
The bend, rippling, flexing,
Clear and endlessly playing,
An innocent muscle gathering motion
To move from beetling bank the imbedded
Black rock:

Pours over the rock,
Oils, anoints the rock
That smoothly wrinkled porpoise brow
Which abuts the clear waters of word.
The rock stands still and still it shapes
The water ahead.

Part II

BAUCIS & PHILEMON

This is that piercing moment, one winter day,
When we have found at last our missing dog
Dead and matted in the roadside ditch;
When the skeletal tree we seldom notice
Suddenly, out of the corner of an eye,
Moves perhaps a single step closer;
When our children at play in a far field
Seem many years older,
Their chests grown big as caves
Where hearts in darkness beat most dreadfully
As the tree of death outside
Moves perhaps a single step closer.

The sky fills with blackbirds whispering by,
A long swarm composing itself on the tree
Which stands up bare as the veins of a leaf.
They pause and then divide, half of them falling
On matted brown grass to feed.
Each time these shift their ground
Like wind blown leaves,
A few more drop to their midst
From the harsh black foliage of the tree.

We crouch here quietly side by side,
Two dark caverns in a sheer cliff,
Two beating, branching culs de sac,
While daylight rages outside.

SHIPS GATHERED TO RESCUE

Beacon lights
Dip on our masts all night,
But the drowning in phosphorous hair
Are forever over there—
Seem to flutter beside a ship
From which they blunderingly slip.

Lifted as though by arms beneath,
They rise to burst into arms
That more than reach,
That rend
When on arms that float like a wreath
Fall arms that bend—

They have all gone under
Yet call and cough;
The rescued sit,
Glisten in gangways
Where we sway or pitch
And take on the shine of their cloth.

GREGORIUS IN INSULA

The gulls of nesting season
Have left, leaving on rocks above
Their bits of shell,
White as a crust of salt
Below at the sea—and, midway, I
Am one white tatter, caught.

The waves upon the surface,
The fish in schools beneath
Must move in the slow progression
Of, far above, the geese—
Making way for a canopy of air
Which they bear in majesty over the sea.

LIKE PINOCCHIO

Your white house leans from the dark
And that wax white, far off you,
Leaning from the window,
Has hair that hangs down all blue.

The long grass stems that tilt and cross
Above the cricket's breathing back
Are whirring in this wind,
Are, in this starlight, grey and black.

You have quietly closed your window
And I loiter here below.
A black night beetle cracks against my knee:
I am jointed like Pinocchio.

Assassins will come as charcoal sacks
And hang me in an oak to jerk and spin.
Brittle as slate or a cricket's shell,
My feet will clatter all night in the wind.

AWAY

After a day's talk
Which wavered gently
About our gentle thoughts—
Ha! as a conscript slashed to blindness
Avoids the dead
And slowly foots across
What soon will be
The most familiar tufted field
He ever crossed—
We parted, uneasy with our words,
Our smiles unhealed.

A WORLD OF WATCHFULNESS

This quiet, briar filled wire,
The ingrown fencing of a pasture
So simply left that from its center
The edge seems unreal as an outer coast,
Has no tautness.
Hanging by its vines
From loose barked, logy posts
Which lie against the sky like spires,
It is difficult to climb.

When from the strangeness of inner space
I watch the wind struck weeds
Which dip toward the fence and, rooted, scatter,
Or the shadows of gulls
That on some brilliant wake
Bounce like leaves
While their gulls on wind wheel, freely, flatter;
When, half looking from under my brow,
I see a woman approach and chatter,
Forget herself in excited ease
And, shifting from her left to right leg, shorter,
Smile from a gently bobbing head—
This field seems the center
Of all I have watched, confused, not said.

THE NIGHT HORSE

I awake an hour before dawn
And still she grazes there,
Slipped somewhere out of the field of sight
But ripping and chewing spring grass
Which grows longer now, gaining momentum:
After the first low hesitant start
It pours forth from the ground
Almost as fast as rain went in.
The horse grazes on the edge of attention;
Half between sleep and feigning sleep,
I dare not look too close or she will go.
Now that there are leaves the wind blows
Like a bear turning over from sleep—
Stirs and rustles and goes.
Silence then, the horse I cannot see
Grazing in the dark at the edge of the woods.
If I could go to her as simply
As the single night song of a bird
Reaches out of the woods—
Reach for her mane and be on her back—
The wind turns over, dawn begins
And the babble of many small birds.

DAYBREAK

Confused at daybreak in a broken dream,
I gazed at my cavernous room
While a hound outside in the voice of morning
Dinned as steadily as a bell.
Cold mist, cold clamor of hound,
Roamed through the screen of my open window,
Compelled my shivering flesh
To rise and watch the daylight swell.

My senses turned unwillingly out:
Agile and blue by the cornfield fence,
A farmer prodded something of fur
To the verge of his seething hound.
The wrongly bulky little beast,
Crabbéd on misty ground,
Became a raccoon released from a trap
To teach the leaping dog its teeth.

Curious steers came circling in
From hazy provinces—to thrust
Uneasy heads in the salty din.
Slowly, slowly the brightening farm
Turned on its pin of distress
Until one stroke of the farmer's stick
Broke open the animal snout.
Daylight and the dog spread out.

FROG IN EARLY FALL

Invisible above in dense white fog
Occasional geese
Utter their confident cries
That pock the marshy silence
Like logs within the river,
Sliding by.

Frog, frog,
Fat green nugget of earth
Exactly as cold as this cold water and fog,
If I squat to hold you in my hands—
Ten minutes of meddlesome warmth
From a warm and alien kingdom—

You would nudge and wriggle free,
Resume your trance among fallen leaves
That creep the watery shore;
Frog, frog,
Enthroned on legs and clever of eye,
You crown and miter cold tidal mud

As geese roam over in early fog.

CARDINAL

Grey and rose she lies in my hand,
Wings smooth to her sides,
A little beating sac like an amulet
Loose from the base of her throat.
The children turn out doors in this whirling wind
To think her now their faithful pet,
But the cat has ripped her past saving.
I cover her with my other hand
And in that pod conceal her death
As in the darkest cedar remote.

FILM

I sit at last in the narrow seat,
Soothed among strangers,
Sick of hearing myself talk,
Thinking, as the lights grow dim,
I am a fool.
Oh masters, monsters, friends,
Relent from my liver and lungs;
I confess it:
Film is better than life.

That running man, there,
Half a block away in my brain—
A trick of blackness, gulping
The distance before him, healing behind—
Trips a hidden land mine of pigeons.
They explode and wheel among buildings;
He keeps on pumping his legs
As though he on his stepped up pavement
And they in their flakes of light
Were struggling, lifting,
Wringing him away
To confess his life.

COMFORT

When in the haste of heartiness
I snatch up a few words,
Smile, and off they fare,
Old friend, beware of my pomposity.
I am so uneasy with another heart's care
I cannot keep a quiet watch
At any side
For fear of the latter moment
When, sideways,
With hopeless, believing eyes,
A face looks up for me
On the last strength of a throat
Needing—what?—pure love like air,
And I find I am not there.

SNOW BLINDNESS

The crust of this temperate portion of earth
Has swollen all day and all night
Two feet thicker with snow.
A cross section now would show
On layers of bedrock, marl, and clay
The minute umber graves of loam
Surmounted by sudden epethelial growth.
Round black boles of trees
Bristle at every angle
And birds therein live vividly on hope.

The freeze holds day after day;
Slowly the roads are cleared
And all the birds of this covered land
Seem to cluster there weakening,
Killed by cars, feeding on grit.
A blackbird in a coasting fall
Ends on his back in powdery snow
Under the stabbing beak of a mockingbird
Who will sing through all the moonlit nights
Of summer—if he lives.

Coming inside, gleaming with cold,
A film of snow upon my eyes,
I grope for a moment,
Reclaim the borders of my head,
Think it the easiest virtue I ever knew
To throw feed for gathering birds
On the bare dirt floor of an open shed—
That noted through summer ways
They may go hedgehopping, flying,
Singing, and finding about my house all day.

Awake in the night, I hear my brain stir,
Feeding on doubt behind my eyes:
How do you say that in a dazzling world
Of new snow, you move in the dark,
In the house, hands stretched out
To fend away a door opening the wrong way,
The corner of a table the size of a grave,
Steps, a fragile chair, any onrushing thing
Forgotten from the blueprint confronting your mind
So close it wraps you in
Closer than your own skin?

As though the poster in a comedy, slapped
On the face of a bystander with miraculous glue,
Had melted without a trace through skin
To invisibly seal off the brain behind eyes.
What then, what do you do—
Hilarious figure—daubed, stumbling
With poster and insoluble glue?
Better to stop, affect an air
That it isn't there, or you aren't there,
Merge with a wall and think the thing through:

Though you are in a panic to be free
You cannot wake the sleeping house,
Cannot fight your way out.
Besides, what good would it do
To regain the world of light
Which, a little too loud and cheerful,
You have always blundered through?
Whatever the film that impedes your eyes,
Dark in light, light in dark,
Is one layer of the blinding skin you live inside.

Part III

WHO ONCE KEPT STORE

The magnificent racks of winter trees
Bound in my lights ahead
Mile after mile.
Cat's eyes appear and then the cat
Calico crouched by the roadside ditch
Where mice may gather food
As minnows in unearthing tide
Go where the heron bides.

Drive on, drive on, my life is running late;
Behind me whirl the grains of another
And another and another state—
Wherein rage, fear, remorse, or shame
Have blasted circuitous brain.
Someone I never saw will soon turn up
Saying, "I know you, you once kept store."
I remember apples in a gleaming pile,

I remember myself vaguely drifting
—A great grey shark in the aquarium
Of glass, concrete, and feathery time—
While slowly there grew on me like rags
The helplessness of standing hungry and vile
In the sight of all my goods
Which were rosy and sweet
And carefully tended as any child.

Headlights lead the way, transfixing
A hundred places where I am not.
Perhaps someone will soon turn up, saying,
"I know you but where are the wife and child?"
Gone, fled from my noisy wits:
Good grey ships asleep in a narrow bay
Leave black uneasy headlands
Before break of day.

Behind me darkness sooths my traces;
I am in danger now like the sea
Of overreaching a long slow curve of coast
To range wolfish and grey among weeds.
Surely someone will soon appear
Saying, "I know you; arrangements are made;
Here is all the life you will live;
Go; keep store; remember the facts."

PRODIGAL SON

Poor grimy pit of a closing town,
It cradles its citizens
Like so many sacks of gold
Tossed hurriedly down.
Daylight slips from the inner buildings,
Dodders briefly by rain in gutters
And, at the end of a vanishing street,
Shows for a moment as no muddled hag
But the faultless blue pause of heaven
Arrayed behind windy green flags.

At dusk, alone, with winter coming on,
The young man feels nerve enough
In seignorial flesh
To stir the sockets of his bones.
Roaming dumb as an ox with great round eyes
Or a giant fish deep in the swerving
Wind of a hostile city,
He drifts easily past the guard
Of a last few strangers, stilted in twilight,
Who inwardly feed their eyes
On the cast-off flesh of the solid world
Like crabs in the cold ebb tide.

Eastward he sights the harbor,
Black with the hulls and whipping flags
Of his long forgotten native land,
The emerald avaricious sea.

ANALOGUES OF A JUROR

As loving left behind
Like a long dark hall
In sunlight still shades the dazzled mind
With parallel walls,
So the life in which you wound us
All summer in darkest thrall
Still shadows me here in fog
Though we sent you to hang last fall.

As a beast ensnared from his runway
Will hang and heavily thrash,
Writhe until others channeled below
Hardly see his solider brown
Through wind rummaged grass,
You were wound in wind and grass while I, I,
I went the way you felt when you murdered—
Left with a love which gibbered inside.

But as marble seems solid in wastes of fog,
I then set loving up like graven law,
Rigged my rights as a jury
To press for the reddest blood I could draw.
Such rights are rapacious, eager to serve
For all their wavering mob.
Daunted still they persist
As ghosts of my going, white in the fog.

SHE SEES PALLBEARERS COMING ON SNOW

If, instead of taking away,
They lifted your long white body dead
And bent it with the strain
Of stringing an unstrung bow,
Bent it until inward cold sinews gave
And it broke at the sockets of your legs—

You would sit then and I
Would sit behind and to one side,
Avoid the field of your eyes
And, thinking us alive,
Would watch your cheek where the beardness shows.
For once you go white into frozen ground
This patch of stubble will grow
Upward, upward, to melt your fine grained snow.

NEAR BUT WHO?

Mountains, cold wind, and snow:
Even the bird of flapping in fields,
The know-all, brass tacks crow,
Here glides the ravines alone
And is the only blackness
In all the shades of snow.

A slender, nervous man
With a barked brown suitcase
Light in his hand
Walks the road which winds in spurts
Across the edge of another country,
Of a language learned, a kind of worth.
He is impossible to place—
Was talked of once in nasal cockney,
Feels safest when, high,
He can look down and say:
"The approaches are free of any spy."
(While here in the cold
His lips purse up in crazy pedantry.)
Skinny, odd, an almost translucent grey,
He was seen a week ago
In Paris—on a bench in the metro.

He who has left a dozen countries—
Sometimes because he was paperless,
Sometimes because he was Jew,
Sometimes because he feared his fear
Of another paperless and Jewish
Yet unexplainable eye—
Sat and rubbed his shiny hard shoes
With a flap of poster
Skinned from the subway wall.
Half fascinated
By a woman's flimsy earrings
Worn thin at the joints from joggling,

He stood to fasten in front
A jacket too small
For even that tiny trunk,
Arranged in his upper pocket
A square of polka-dot cloth
And looked out wondering, near,
From a face of too narrow glasses, of mouth
And too large ears.

Again enroute from somewhere
He sat one early June
On a hill above Florence
(While bugle, bell, and birds
Figured the upper air
Of a clear blue noon)
And thought of himself in the scene
With a Renaissance cape
Of scarlet, black, and gold.
Embroidered more than stitched at the seams,
It should arrange itself resting
In wonderful landscape folds.
Yet those arms would flurry it oddly,
And a well loved ravine
Still show his contraction knobby.

He is so courteous, cautious, and queer
That all who have harried him long
Must have felt themselves changed
To an austere dream of tongs
Chasing an ash which rises through flames
To brilliantly dip—and disappear.

KORÊ TO COED

(Archaic Smile to Youthful Scorn)

A proper fledgling blown awry,
You wear the foolish look, my dear, not I.
Burly and cross on a windy branch
That somehow found your feet,
My sister, my sparrow, be chipper.
Get you a fitting smile to your cheek
While breezes nibble and the year is weak.
A venerable wind is shifting afar
To uphold your fitful wings
And gull you forever of a timid heart.
Midway in the migration of your life,
With substance of flesh grown secretly thin
In a most fruitful year,
You must bear in the steady wind
My beakéd smile from ear to ear.

AT BAY

in memory, R. J.

Inhale, respire,
The silence all around
Sucks like a steady wind
At one small chance of fire.
Grey stump growing thin
While working loam crumbles away
Within, and year after year
A crackling beard of honeysuckle
Prowls about.
The volcanic skin of the human world
Wrinkles and crawls;
Craterous, miles of habitation
Grow thin in the walls.

A poem used to take hold like a fist within,
Draw back, draw back,
And fling you forever beyond the walls.
But the stone grew up like iron again,
You had to gather your strength,
Hold yourself straight and hopeful—
Talk, translate, try anything
To keep people amiable, uninterrupting
While you waited,
Preserving that dangerous silence
Which quivered within:
At any moment it might uproot
And fling you forever beyond the walls.

BED RIDER

Strength was once my stand
I think and having thought,
Draw my lids against the leaning of a wall.
I see myself implant a foot
On the hatchmarks of a broad brown floor—
Which slips aside as though to dance
One matronly measure on the side of a wave
Before blundering into the trough.

I settle sideways
Into a sea of darkness
Which must diminish me like sleep
To powers I never lost—
For when someone opens at daylight
A door in my head
The room and I flap hugely once
Like a drowning moth.

All day my legs lie sunken in cloth.
My forearms crossed upon my chest
Are helves the women put aside
While with their fingers and their biddy eyes
They tend my body like a garden.
Its crops are more dreadful than dust—
And there at night reopen the craterous sores
Which they discuss.

Scritch-scratch, scritch-scratch they go
And in each abrasion they savor
The barren outermost lands
I long ago lost—
Old cabbage head tossed in a sea
Of senseless, solitary fault,
I feel the water lapping, loosening
The innermost leaves of my thought.

FALL PLANTING

She digs and digs,
Grown wiry with her loss of life.
The rich cold mealy earth
Under the blade of her shovel
Is wiry with grass.
All afternoon
Fat bulbs in their papery skins
Two by two, six inches deep
Sink in.

Behind her back
The sheds are beginning to rear
And play in the wind
Like young goats.
The walls of her house tug,
Tug to go free,
To ride like a long slow wave
This rise above the river
Where they first took hold.

Her mother lies inside,
Tangled in Christmas cactus,
Plucking her mind,
Softly, softly,
One dove at a time
Until all she can say
To the daughterly face above her,
Straining to keep great baby alive,
Is "I'm dying, I'm dying."

Old wounds in the porch screening
Are sutured with self wire.
Geese on the river
Mutter like sleep,
Cedar hoards redbirds,
Elm gibbers to sky,
And one high window pipes in the wind
The wandering song
Of a goatboy to his flock.

Hounds yell through the woods for deer.
Faintly, upstream, gravel machines
Eat the river shore,
As they have feasted, fed barges
For the past two years.
She digs and digs into silence
For flowers, must feed her mother.
The rich cold wind covers her ears
For hours.

EMINENCE IN AUCTION HALL

Agate set in bronze, I watch and buy
The pedestalled head of an ancient god,
Head full of silence and halted corrosion
Daunting the room with empty eyes.
I draw my skin down tight
Inside the finest wool in the world—

As the flocks of Greece go piping by
I come upon the head all wanderers hope for,
Some perfection of place which no one has robbed:
Unknown headwaters of a thousand miles of river,
Say, or simply a greenish knob, almost another rock
On the rocky verge of a spring gone dry.

I knock and pry until it breaks loose,
Turns at last in the sunlight, and is prized.
Hunched like a predator, I carry my head to the shade,
There tap forth the stubborn interior clod
Which holds the agate eyes and ruined features
Of my pitted hollow god.

My wife at my side, her younger hair fluffed
To her face, dissociates herself from my decline.
Corrosion grows its crystals silently,
Taking old substance as temporary shape,
Drawing the bronze skin finer and finer
Until it collapses of its own light weight.

Head full of ruined power, prized in this hall,
I still know who to smile upon and bless,
Who, just slightly less, to smile upon
And when he stands to receive at my eyes
His momentary, life-long caress,
To never see at all.

CATHEDRAL TOWN

Slowly a tower bell swings into wind,
Its great round burr of voice
Blown rolling back from the river brim—
A swimmer beats forth
Until he spins, he rings
On a current so clear blue and thin
It welcomes his coming
As a high birdcry is welcomed by wind.

Here shattering rocks dispel
The fragile darks of day:
Shadows and the brooding bell
Which stirred him peacefully hitherward
Were, in the woodland park,
Changing and arranging
Their shy, uneasy grace
Around all that in his mind
Went wayward wingéd angeling.

Now suddenly wrecked, his body lies
As limp on rock as soon it will lie
On a back rounded to the burden
Of close and heavy flesh that has died.
The bell in the streaming air above
Must shoulder once more
The ponderous question of flesh and blood:
Has he cleaved the clouds of the rapid sky;
Is he welcomed, wingéd, high?

LONG VOYAGE HOME

Old rubbish man, so here you are,
With both hands clenched to the rail,
Still working the wing bones in your back
While a long dark ridge of homeland
Slides closer and closer to your knee
Like a wary hound.

Here you are to be cherished at last
As though you had spent your life
In a house behind those trees;
As though your land dipped and rolled
And rose with olive trees
Before on this farther side
It fell off twenty fathoms
To a narrow passage where ships may glide.

Your few possessions quickly stored,
You will take up residence with yourself
Like a doubtful brother,
Rummaging to waste and confusion
The magnificent chest of all you surely know:

You who have rumbled daily to the top of a mound
Whereby a storied town moves against the marsh
With all the rubbish at its command.
Everything here lives in extremity.
Rats, dogs, a scavenging man,
Pause, hide, look the other way,
Deny to themselves that you arrive
With a big white load of hope.
You can see for miles from the top of the dump
Where a high dusk mothers the sullen smoke.
Beyond the marsh grey water slides
And ships nuzzle the wharves
An old city extends.

Wrong, wrong, wrong again.
Polished, translucent, and perfectly hinged
To outlast the invention of the hour,
Plastic boxes crackle underfoot
With the delicate armor plate of vermin
Living, defenseless, in their final bower.

Surefooted and happy you hold out your hand.
The ramp rattles down, your voyage ends.

THUS EVER TO TYRANTS

Says
Words are cheap, says
What do you want me to say?
I'll say it, I'll say it.
I am other than a voice
I live in a cave
The light comes and goes.
What do you want from me
Who inhabits darkness
Darkly?
Who never did anything to you
But deal in words
When forced to deal,
As water weeds
Coming to the mouth of the pool
Are forced to deal in leaves
For the sake of the fingering roots
Out of sight.

Back down in there
I am nothing to you.
But as we grow,
Rising, laboring,
Slaves of the tyrannous light,
Do not abuse me.
I do not know why,
But if you come one step closer—
Even though we are of the one flesh
And will be mingled together
In darkness forever—
I will lay you open
From gut to gullet
In one great red lolling
Blossom of a sunlit smile.

NOWHERE

It happens all the time:
A man will leave his house
One winter morning in the usual way,
The cold knob clings an instant to his hand,
The least twig of the smallest bush
Is stiff in the dazzling light.
A clear path of his old footprints
Breaks the ripples of the frozen snow
But he has loitered too long inside:
The nearest figure is far away.
He goes to speak and in his mouth
He finds a foreign tongue, fumbling
Outlandish familiar words
With all the gestures of the acutely dumb.
Hundreds of thousands of gallons
Of cold still air
Shout in his alien ears
Fit themselves to his face
Funnel
Pour in
Flood him away in a language
He never knew before, his own
Dazzling black roar.